D1326126

Withdrawn From Stock
Dublin City Public Libraries

To my mother, Gerri, for her endless love

JANETTA OTTER-BARRY BOOKS

Text and photographs copyright © Suzi Eszterhas 2014

The right of Suzi Eszterhas to be identified as the author and photographer of this work
has been asserted by her in accordance with the Copyright, Designs and Patents Act, 1988
(United Kingdom).

First published in Great Britain and in the USA in 2014 by
Frances Lincoln Children's Books, 74-77 White Lion Street, London N1 9PF
www.franceslincoln.com

All rights reserved

No part of this publication may be reproduced, stored in a retrieval system, or transmitted,
in any form, or by any means, electrical, mechanical, photocopying, recording or otherwise
without the prior written permission of the publisher or a licence permitting restricted copying.
In the United Kingdom such licences are issued by the Copyright Licensing Agency,
Saffron House, 6-10 Kirby Street, London EC1N 8TS.

A catalogue record for this book is available from the British Library.

ISBN 978-1-84780-503-4

Set in Stempel Schneidler

Printed in China

1 3 5 7 9 8 6 4 2

ELEPHANT

Suzi Eszterhas

F

FRANCES LINCOLN
CHILDREN'S BOOKS

Pembroke Branch Tel. 6689575

Far away, in the grasslands of Africa, a baby elephant is born. He is born with pink eyes and pink feet, and the backs of his ears are pink too. Over time they will change from pink to grey. The baby is called a calf and he is very wobbly and slow when he walks. His mum keeps him safe and close under her big belly.

Leabharlanna Poibli Chathair Baile Átha Cliath

Dublin City Public Libraries

The elephant mother cuddles her baby by touching him with her trunk. This is like a really long nose that can also be used as an arm or a hand. She wraps her big trunk around his little trunk to give him an 'elephant hug'. The rest of the elephant family are also excited about the new baby and they touch him with their trunks, too.

The calf is one of the biggest baby animals in the world. He weighs hundreds of kilograms but still looks tiny next to his mother. She is careful to keep him close at all times, and she protects him from danger with her huge body.

Elephant calves are always hungry. To grow strong and healthy, calves need plenty of their mother's milk and are always ready to fill their tummies. The calf will grow very slowly. It will take him 15 years to grow up to be one of the largest animals on earth.

The calf has a very close family of aunts, sisters, brothers and cousins. His mother is the oldest female and the leader of the group. The family is always together and the mothers will even look after each other's calves. If trouble comes too close, the adults will form a circle round the calves to keep them safe.

It gets very hot on the African grasslands, and the family must be careful to keep cool. The shade of a tree makes the perfect place to escape the heat and take a nap. Flapping their huge ears like fans also helps to keep the elephants cool. And their tough, wrinkled skin protects them from the hot sun.

Leabharlanna Poibli Chathair Baile Átha Cliath
Dublin City Public Libraries

The elephant family needs water. The elephants must drink water nearly every day to stay healthy. They love to lie in the mud to cool down. Splashing around in the water is also fun and, if the water is deep, the calves can use their trunks as snorkels.

At the age of four, the calf's tusks are getting bigger. His tusks are like big teeth, and they will continue to grow throughout his life. The calf is learning how to use his tusks to dig up plants and trees to eat. He also uses them when playing with other calves. One day he may need to use them to protect himself.

In the dry season, sometimes it does not rain for months. Then the family must travel far to find good grass to eat. Along the way, they meet up with other families and travel in a big group, called a herd. Elephants have amazing memories, and during the journey they will see old friends they have travelled with before. They may also meet new elephant friends.

The elephant spends lots of his time play-fighting with other young males. They use their heavy bodies and tusks to crash into each other, and they playfully hit each other with their trunks. This is fun, but it also helps the elephant build strength and confidence, so that he can be brave and defend himself when threatened.

After 12 years the elephant is nearly grown-up. He now knows elephant language. He can use his trunk to make loud trumpeting sounds. But he can also make low rumbling noises that make the ground slightly shake. Other elephants can feel this with their feet and trunks – even many miles away.

Male elephants grow more and more curious about the world outside the family. Now that he is completely grown-up, it is time for the young elephant to leave his family.

Female elephants will stay with their families forever, but all male elephants will leave to explore the world on their own. Travelling alone, they may walk over a hundred miles in a single day.

Now the elephant uses all the skills his mother and family have taught him. He knows where to find the most delicious grass to eat. He knows where to find water or how to dig for it during very dry times. And he knows how to chase off animals that are a danger to him.

After many days of roaming the plains on his own, he is happy to meet another male elephant. They quickly become friends. They will travel together and they will eat, drink and bathe together. They will even give each other 'elephant hugs'. Sometimes they will meet up with other male elephants, but these two elephants will remain best friends for the rest of their lives, even after fathering calves of their own.

Leabharlanna Poibli Chathair Baile Átha Cliath
Dublin City Public Libraries

More about Elephants

- Elephants live in Africa and Asia.

- Elephants are the largest of all land animals. Adult males, called bulls, can weigh up to 6.35 tonnes (14,000 pounds). That's as heavy as a school bus!

- Elephants can get sunburned, so they need to throw sand and mud on their heads and backs to protect themselves. The wrinkles in their skin help the mud and sand stick to their skin, providing a layer of natural sunscreen and insulation from the heat.

- Elephants can recognise themselves in the mirror, a skill shared only with humans, apes, magpies and dolphins.

- The low rumbling (seismic) communication of elephants can travel up to 10 miles along the ground.

- An elephant can drink 225 litres of water a day.

- An elephant's trunk contains 100,000 muscles and tendons, giving it extreme flexibility and strength.

- Elephants are matriarchal, which means that female elephants always lead the family groups. Male elephants live mainly on their own, joining up with females only to mate with them.

- Elephants can live to be 70 years old.

- Elephants are endangered because people hunt them for their tusks, which are made of valuable ivory and used for carvings in Asia.

- For more information visit www.elephantvoices.org